ALLOWING

MY HEART

TO BEAT

DIFFERENTLY

Book of Poems

C.L. Suggs

ISBN: 978-1-7375700-1-1

Library of Congress Cataloging-in-Publication data: TXu2-282-193. Revised Version
Requested information should be addressed to
P O Box 953 Winterville, (NC) 28590

www.changerequireschange.org
or
www.crcinternationalministries.com

Editor: Linda Samuel
Designer: Vinny Gazzara

Printed in the United States of America

Introduction

I often said that during the many trials and tribulations of my life, hate wanted to surround me, but I am thankful that love found me. Mercifully, love turned me around and into a better person. If we study the rhythms of the heart, it beats differently regarding the changes we all go through. The various changes of love, hate, fear, rejection, pain, grief, happiness, and the like. What we allow ourselves to go through will determine intense feelings of the heartbeat. It is easy to fall into bitterness, but we must become better, not bitter. I made the conscious decision to allow my heart to beat differently as I govern it accordingly. Each poem is a part of my heart beating inversely.

C.L. Suggs expresses in her writing from the flow of her heart, and she celebrates and cherishes her existence as she has experienced and discovered it. Emotion is a basic need that God has gifted us all with, but we shouldn't let our emotions rule us. All the tears that run down our faces, we have to decide will it be tears of sadness or tears of joy. *Allowing my heart to beat differently* is an account of heart inspirations, revelations, and interactions with self, life, and people.

When we think about love, it is all about chemicals of deep attractions to their logical sources. The physiological arousal of one vibe is linked to the next. Have you ever noticed when you had a certain crush, it caused your heart rate to increase, perspire, or nerves jacked up all over the place? Well, it can be traced back to the chemical balance of an adrenaline rush. Think about the time that God did above and beyond what we asked. Our heartbeat will speak the joys on our faces. We can learn so much from a heartbeat. Our emotions which are linked to our feelings can make one feel either optimistic, energetic, focused, motivated, stressed, depressed, oppressed, and so much more. So, whatever you may feel as you read each poem – remember you have the control to govern your mind, body, and actions.

I pray these poems will bless you as you read them.

POEMS

LIFE

Though I struggle with life and problems

I can always trust You

Even though things do not go the way I perceive

But Your way is always sure and true

Father, I can always run to safety in You

You never shame me, act unseemly or cruel

Thank You for all the ways You've made

Because if You didn't, I'll probably be in the grave

You gave me a wonderful Savior

To enjoy and give great favor

Father, thank You for this abundant life

Even in this warring fight

With confidence, I can truly say, this battle is already won

It was won the day I accepted Your Holy Son

Love always and forever your daughter/son, _____ (put

your name there).

Daughter of Zion

LOVE

Be who you are, and all God called you to be,

Don't limit yourself to be in bondage but accept the

gift to be free

Share your heart with the right one, who knows God's love and

does not wonder

Neither of you will be limited to the blessings above

but know how to treat one another like a dove

God has so much in store for us all to obtain,

But wait patiently for God, so that you're not in a strain

Always know we need each other to survive,

Yes, there are up days and down days but, God will revive

We only live once so live to the best that God has chosen

Love your family, neighbors, and enemies as

you would a red rose

Remember red represents the blood of Jesus Christ,

The one who loves you and gave His life

If you don't remember anything from this day,

I'm here to say, that God loves you... in a very special way.

CHOSE TO BE A VOICE

We have no choice of how we come into this world

But we do have a choice of how we leave this world

Don't leave out the same way you came in

You can be free from this world and the power of sin

You are somebody

No if, and, but, or probably

Jesus died for all

Not race, sex, or statue of being short or tall

He rains on the just as well as the unjust

You are here raised from the dust

Giving His breath of life

So, you don't have to live in strife

It is your choice to have abundant life

Or you can just keep existing and soon die

Make the right choice

And be His voice

A voice that declares

That Jesus loves you and He cares

A voice that says, though you slay me, yet will I trust you

Knowing that He didn't call all …only chose a few

A voice that binds and loose strongholds

To discern spirits of things foretold

A voice that decrees all things are working together

That is why I can encourage my sister and my brother

A voice that states I can do all things through Christ

For it is He who strengthens me even when I cry

A voice that says Satan bring your best shot

Because no weapon will prosper not even your plot

A voice that stands up for the truth

Even if I have to be rebuked

A voice that not only speaks with my mouth

But showing deeds with my hands going north, east,

west and south

I will be His voice

Because I made the choice

For God, I live and for God, I die

When it's over in His bosom shall I lie

I made a choice to be His voice

Will you be His voice?

Will you be His voice?

Sometimes the voice has to stand up against mom and dad

Sister or brother

Husband or wife or even a neighbor

Sometimes the voice has to stand up against false Pastors,

Bishops, and Apostles

Elders or even Elderess, Priest and Prophets

Yeah, whatever one wishes to call themselves using selfish

gains as profits

Sometimes the voice has to stand up against the

flesh we live in

To allow the Holy Spirit to win

Be His voice

Be His voice

Be His voice

ASK YOURSELF A QUESTION

?

Yes, every man has fallen

But only the good ones get back up

They realize whose hands they are holding

Man says life is hard

Jesus said life is easy

What is the difference one may ask?

Jesus was willing to please His Father

Man is willing to please others

Jesus said, "I am the way"

Why the way?

Salvation is the only way to see the Kingdom

Jesus said, "I am the truth"

Why the truth?

Because it is impossible to please Him without knowing

Jesus said, "I am the life"

Why the life?

Because you must die to gain eternal life

It's not hard to be born again

It is hard when we refuse to die to our sins

Every man has fallen

Only the good ones get back up

They realize whose hands they are holding

Is your hand in God's or man's?

Here is a secret that you must remember

God will pull you back up through repentance

Man will set you up through the spirit of distance

I'll rather have my hands in the Master's hand

Than Satan's who doesn't know the eternal plan

Ask yourself a question?

Who is holding your hands?

DON'T GIVE UP

We are just tourists passing through

Open your eyes and admire the view

Many have come to places in their life

They wanted to give up and die

But keep pressing through all the stress and mess

I promise you; soon you'll have the best

Don't give up on your dreams

No matter how bad it seems

We all live in a world

With so many different boys and girls

Living life is not a burden

It's a guide to joy-filled living

Don't give up on your dreams

No matter how bad it seems

Stay focus and in those books

No excuse they have iPads, E-readers, and Nooks

Many say knowledge is power

But the truth is, you have to apply it like soap in a shower

Nothing is impossible to those who believe

Because those are the one's who always receive

Don't give up on your dreams

No matter how hard it seems

Yes, I know somethings have knocked you down

But it's your choice to get up or stay bound

We all can decide to give up or pursue

Even I made a decision to get up and do

Doing something with my talents, gifts, and time

Even if I have to start saving every dime

No test, trial, or situation is easy or a piece of pie

It is up to you to confront it, learn from it, or continue to live a

lie

So, no matter what life may throw your way

Be like a tourist; pass through, but don't stay

Don't stay in the same mess year after year

Get up and do something beneficial my dear

For one, don't give up on your dreams

No matter how bad it seems

WE WILL NOT FEAR

When I was younger, I use to be terrified of bees

Not just bees but snakes that slithered through the leaves

Even now as an adult some of those things still terrify me

Of course, not as bad as being a child but it still affects me

I remember when a bee flew into my house

I was so afraid I would have rather had a mouse

I was curling my hair, jumping hysterically; the curlers fell on

my face

Running from a bee, that left me with a scar, that I can't escape

Man, was it even worth it?

I should've stood still eventually it would've flown away

Or I could've swat it with nothing left to say

I think about my children who should be afraid of nature but

not mankind

Shall we raise our generation to live in fear,

And not allow their authenticity to shine?

I refuse to teach my children to be afraid of authority and white

supremacy

However, I will teach them to trust the Master who

has all authority

This is not the life we envisioned

Running, standing still, eating, and still getting killed

No, this is not the life we envisioned,

Yet still teaching our kids about life in the midst of a pandemic

This is not the life we envisioned as we continue to suffer from

historical trauma due to our race

This is not the life we envisioned saying we surrender

But, still getting killed like a body thrown in a grinder

This is not the life we envisioned seeing the news and crying

because another brother or sister of color keeps dying

Man, oh man... God this is not the life we envisioned

It's even scarier for those that have been imprisoned

Many are getting out and going back to penitentiary

They realize there are no rules or regulations for their safety

Nevertheless, we make this our decree

"We will not live in fear"

Because we know that is definitely not the plan of

God my dear

We will walk confidently in who we are, even

when it seems unfair

Because we realize our kind is something special and very rare

We will not walk in fear

MY HEART AND MY JOY

When a loved one dies it is always painful

But when your little one dies it goes beyond normal

Not having the potential to experience a full life

But God had a plan that was not with strife

They say it is amazing how a mom stays so strong

Knowing you will never see your little one for long

Before saying your goodbyes

Still not truly understanding why

Time is slowly healing the wounds year after year

But I will always miss you, my dear

Most days it's easy to say I'm ok

Instead of telling people what I really want to say

I love you, baby boy

You are my heart and my joy

If it were possible that I could visit heaven for a day

Maybe for a moment, my pain would go away

Life can be unkind especially when hearts are torn into shreds

But nothing will ever compare to the pain of losing you

The love you left behind

Will forever live in my heart as a sign

I love you, baby boy

You are my heart and my joy

Keep God smiling now that you are back in your destined place

Keep sending me kisses at night on my lovely face

Assuring me that you are ok

And soon I'll see you and we will have much to say

Until the day we see each other face to face

I will always love you, baby boy

You are my heart and my joy

To Natasha Cannon. In memory of her son, J. Cannon

THE HAND WITH THE PEN

At one point in my life, I viewed celebrities and actors as if they

had it all together

But self-realization let me know even they have a writer

Throughout every movie and story, we see

How we think others may have transformed to be

Did we ever consider, if any credit goes to the scriptwriter?

If truth be told no credit goes to the back scene only those that

are seen

As we all stand in awe of the plays and acts

that are being played

Not thinking or considering the writer whose

mind has been raid

Can we give credit to the hand with the pen

that made it all so?

He/she is the real hero, so cool, so dope, and on the low

Even as I ponder about human life sometimes

How we try to take credit is one prime

Do we even give credit to our great Creator?

The One who knows how each story end, but still is willing to

be the mediator

Sadly, there're times we snatched the pen out of His hands

Because we thought we could write better

Only allowing ourselves to go through so many unnecessary

trials and errors

He is the only One that can write the best love letters

From the beginning to the ending making us all better

Ask yourself a question-Whose hand is the pen in now

Still wondering who or you really don't know who

Daily asking yourself how your life will turn out

Well, that is the first indicator that your ink is about to run out

Put the pen in the hands that know the hairs on your head

If I can make a suggestion, do it now before you go to bed

Please understand that life is not guaranteed to you or me

But we can be the righteous fruit from the Living tree

Ah man, I wish you'll put the pen in His hand

He'll write the best-selling story, as well as make you a better

woman/man

Your ink will run out soon

Just like your life that is running off fumes

God is the best writer and wants to write your story

Because He affirms one day, you will give Him glory

Contrastly, there is a difference in having the hand with just a

writer's pen

And having the right hand with the keeper's pen

You choose whose pen writes this story,

But I promise you, God will eventually get the glory

His ink will never run out and you will never have to wonder

or doubt

When the pen is put in the Master's Hand

THE ROADS ARE
BLACK AND WHITE

As we ride down most roads, we realize most

are black and white

No other color is ever seen in sight

As we ride, we see the white never dominates the black

But the black overpowers even the cracks

We ride down these roads, realizing all of them

need construction

Not one more than the other, but each in transition

As we ride down these roads, it

never argue whose riding me

It's only the humans in the vehicles with the problems we see

As we ride down these roads, we view many signs of warning

Some humans intentionally break them, then get in court lying

As we continue to ride these roads, will anything ever change

with the color codes

People steadily making their own rules and ignoring the main

color of the roads

As we ride these roads, I'm reminded that the first shall be last

And the last shall be first all because of our heinous past

As we ride these roads, know there is a King

that is seen on the highway

One who never sleeps or slumber and judge everything, and

don't play

As we ride these roads remember you own nothing

Not even the dingy signs that you think is something

As we ride these roads, be conscious that black always

dominates the white

Maybe that is why we are always seeing road fights

As we ride these roads don't let competition control you

Not even the one in authority can keep the accurate patrol

As we ride these dark roads, please do not abort

But pray, be respectful, and have a voice in court

As we ride these roads, we have to trust the Higher one

He's the only one that can keep us, so please don't run

As we ride these roads, remember what you see

Always see greater, see freedom, see being yourself

As we ride these roads never let anyone

dictate where you shall be

Sit down, write your vision, and make it plain- is the true key

As we ride these roads, the destination could be limitless

Don't ever let anyone take away that trueness

As we ride these roads that we see every day in sight

Remember, the roads are black and white

PRAY FOR GOD'S BLESSINGS

When you are feeling lonely

I pray for Jehovah's blessings of love

When you are feeling sad

I pray for Jehovah's blessing of joy

When you are feeling discouraged

I pray Jehovah's blessings of hope

When your spirit is to its lowest

I pray for Jehovah's blessings of beauty

When you are troubled in spirit

I pray for Jehovah's blessings of peace

When you are in pain

I pray for Jehovah's healing virtue

When you are feeling no one understands

I pray Jehovah will continue to allow you to be original

When you are feeling all have walked away

I pray Jehovah will not allow you to go astray

When you are feeling financially in a mess

I pray Jehovah continues to give you His best

But first, make sure you are walking in obedience

Because that will always give you confidence

That the blessings of Jehovah will come

To those who wait for Him to perform

Performing His great blessings of love

Only from above

WE NEED HIM

They that call upon His name

The same shall be saved

Ask yourself a question

Do you need Him this day?

It does not matter who you are

It does not matter what you are

We all need Him, we all need Him

We all need Him each and every day

Even if it's for healing

We need Him

Even if it's for deliverance

We still need Him

Even if it's for salvation

We definitely need Him

We all need Him each and every day

Even if it's for love

He is love so we need Him

Even if it's for hope

We still need Him

Even if it's for joy

We definitely need Him

We all need Him each and every day

Not only for a moment but every hour, minute, and second of

the day

We can not make it on our own no matter what we say

We can not make it without Him

We all need Jesus each and every day

SPECIAL FRIEND

When you feel like you are all alone

When you feel like there is no one to call on

When you feel like everyone has walked away

Always know, that you have a special friend

He has several names, one being Jesus

His name is also Emmanuel

His name is Prince of Peace

And He wants to meet all your emotional needs

He will never leave you alone

He is always praying on His throne

That is why He is my loving friend

I call on Him morning, noon, and night

He will never leave out of my sight

He is truly a Wonderful Savior

He will stick closer than any brother, and give you divine favor

That is why I can call Him my Shield and Butler

The one that can and will discern all the no-good hustlers

He desires to be your special friend today

Yes, He is my special friend I must say

Wherever and whenever I need Him

He will always be my special gem

He will be your special friend too

All you have to do is call on Him and He'll make you anew

Will you let Him be your special friend today?

TRUST THE EVIDENCE

If God does not love you

Then who can?

If God can not do it

Then who will?

If God did not say it

Then who did?

I'm going to trust the evidence in me

If God does not give you what you have

Who else would?

If God is not your source

Then who is?

If God does not care about your life

Then who would or could?

If Jesus did not die

Then who did?

If the blood did not cleanse us

Tell me what could?

If His power was not transferred

Tell me just what was?

I'm going to trust the evidence in me

If Holy Spirit doesn't guide us

Then who can?

If Holy Spirit doesn't speak

Then how can we interpret revelation?

If Holy Spirit doesn't hear

How can we discern our Father's voice?

If Holy Spirit is not part of the Trinity

Then how are we doing Kingdom work?

Holy Spirit compels us to flee from sin and please God

If you're not pleasing Him; then who are you yielding to?

I'm going to trust the evidence in me because it set me free

REMEMBRANCE

I was born in remembrance of you

I walked the earth in remembrance of you

I was talked about in remembrance of you

I was falsely accused in remembrance of you

I was mocked in remembrance of you

I was betrayed in remembrance of you

I was sold for little in remembrance of you

I became poor in remembrance of you

I was willing to taste the bitter in remembrance of you

I step down in remembrance of you

I was beaten in remembrance of you

I shed my blood in remembrance of you

I was pierced in the side in remembrance of you

I declared it was finished in remembrance of you

I died in remembrance of you

I resurrected with all power in remembrance of you

You were special in my Father's eyes

Before the foundation of the world- there you were

You lost your way, and only I could save you

That is why I took all that, in remembrance of you

Why can't you remember me?

Why can't you see, it was done only through Me

I am your Savior, Friend, Comforter, whatever you

need Me to be

Can you stand to be talked about in remembrance of Me?

Can you stand to be falsely accused in the remembrance of Me?

When they mock you is it in remembrance of Me?

Or just what do they see

Can you give to the poor in remembrance of Me?

Can you sell all you have in remembrance of Me?

Can you tell of my goodness in remembrance of Me?

Can you dwell in praise in remembrance of Me?

Can you worship daily in remembrance of Me?

Can you love in remembrance of Me?

Can you forgive in remembrance of Me?

Can you stand in the midst of the storm in remembrance of Me?

Can you handle the fire in remembrance of Me?

Can you commune without any

iniquity in remembrance of Me?

Can you live in peace and purity in remembrance of Me?

I fulfilled My Father's will in remembrance of you

Now it is time for you to establish and perfect the will in

remembrance of Me

Luke 22:19 says, Do this in remembrance of Me

NOW Think

What if no one said anything to you in a day?

Or even help you along the way

What if no one said anything regarding your good deeds?

Or even saw you had a need

What if no one ever says, "I'm praying for you"?

Or even stop to say, I love you

What if no one ever gave to you?

Or even show any kind of affection to you

Now think about how God feels

He wants to talk to you

Always willing to help you, even when you don't realize it

Waiting to hear His creation/children say thank You

Knowing you had a need and sent His Son to your rescue

Now His only Son sits in heaven praying for you

Always showing His love for all….. not just a few

Giving us each day to cherish and appreciate

Forever showing grace, mercy, and NEVER hesitating

Stop being selfish by thinking of me, myself, and I

Think about how God feels,

Think about how other feels,

Now think about how it makes you feel

I AM HE

Who is He? One may ask?

He is the one that wants you to believe in Him

In the Book of John, we see John the Baptist made the way for
the true light

Nathaniel asked a question, "whence thou knowest me"

It was Jesus that answered and said

Before Phillip called thee when thou were under the fig tree, I
saw thee

Nathaniel said, "thou art the Son of God the King of Israel"

Because I said, "I saw thee under a fig tree and thou believest

Thou shall see greater things than these

If you ever want to see miracles like the first miracles of Cana

Believe that He is He

Jesus knew even with Nicodemus, as with us, we need more than a teacher

We need a Savior

More than religion, we need regeneration

More than the law, we need life

The woman at the well questioned, "Is this the Christ"?

Jesus said unto her, "I that speak unto thee am He"

And the woman said, "now we believe not because of thy saying"

For we have heard Him ourselves, know that is indeed Christ

The Savior of the world

I am He who helped your son in the 7th hour when he openeth his mouth

Miracles will cause you to believe and your whole house

Jesus said this is the work of God, that ye believe on Him whom He sent

I am He that true bread not as your fathers ate and are dead

But I will raise you up in the last day

I am He that speaketh words that are Spirit and Life

Be as the 12, who didn't walk away

but believed and assured that thou are the Christ the Son of the

Living God

John 7:4, "For there is no man that doeth anything in secret

And he himself seeketh to be known openly

If thou do these things show thyself to the world"

So, there was a division among the people because of Jesus

But He saith, he that believeth in Me, as the scripture has said

Out his belly shall flow rivers of living water

I am He who stooped down so you could step up despite your

accusers

I am He the Light of the World

Faith comes before sight and he that heareth God's word is of

God

Even the blind man from birth answered and said

who is He, Lord, that I might believe in Him?

Jesus said unto him, "Thou hast both seen Him and have talked

with thee

He said, Lord, I believe and worshipped Him

I am He that said Mary and Martha if thou wouldest believe

Thou shouldest see the glory of God

I am He that is the Resurrection and Life

And not of that nation only, but that also he should gather

together in one

The children of God that were scattered abroad

Limited faith is controlled by circumstances and motivated by

fear and failure

Faith has to go beyond your cry to the living all-powerful in

Christ

Jesus wept because of limited faith but when she recalled if

thou believest

You shall see the glory of God she wasn't disappointed

You have to believe then we shall see

Be careful that you don't run to what God didn't call you to do

And what He declared us to do we don't do

Stop trying to figure it out, work it out, and just praise it out

For He ....is truly......... He

A GRANDMOTHER'S DREAM

This was a dedication to my grandmother, Catherine

Grandmother, God has blessed you to see 82 years

With seven children, 2 passed away which caused hurt and

tears

Yet God has never left you but continues to bless you

Life has been hard, but God always brought you through

I remember hearing you ask God to take you home

But He has kept you here because He'll never leave you alone

There were times growing up I would hear you sing "At the

Cross"

Being so young I didn't understand just what you saw

You would always say keep me near the cross oh Lord

That when I get to heaven, you'll have my reward

I realize today just what that song means

I too, on Jesus had to lean

I would have failed, truthfully, we all would have failed

But because of God's love, He sent His Son, that none should

go to hell

Grandmother, you have taught me to keep the faith

And the enemy can't do anything without God's say

Yes, your collards, fried chicken, and even your kool-aid was

good

But, God is better than good, and grandma you taught me to

see that goodness

Grandmother's dream is that all her grandkids be saved

And allow Jesus to be all they crave

No one can take back all that has happened in the past

But God desires us to strive for greater future tasks

Coming together is the opening

Keeping together is the kindling

Working together is the settling

One day the small will be great

And just like Grandma, the forgotten will be remembered

And the faithful will be rewarded and honored

And, today, we honor Grandma's dream as we hear her voice

She would always say- no one will force you, but it's your choice

Either enter into glory with me

Or you will depart and go to hell and never be free

THINGS IN LIFE

It is not a shame

But an opportunity

For what we see

And what we can change

We say we're the Body of Christ

But Jesus never ran from a fight

He went in the midst of all trouble

Ready to heal, deliver, and save and give a great double

Let's not just sit and talk about situations

But to move, do, and create great relations

Things in life sometimes seem hard

But Jesus gave us all we need because He is King of kings and

Lord of lords

Let's stop saying it's a shame

For it is not a shame

But an opportunity for what we see

And what we could change

The things in life

PAIN

When pain comes who does it affect

Who does it cause to be affected?

When pain comes it affects everyone that is connected

It causes families and relationships to be disconnected

When pain comes it affects some with tears

When pain comes it affects some with fears

When pain comes it is like a daggering knife

Now, asking why am I here, what's left in this life

Suicide is a factor from hurting pain

Even some mental institutes for people thinking they are insane

Pain comes to shift you out of purpose

But God would rather we lift our hands in worship

When pain comes avoid using a permanent solution

Because the problem is only temporary, and you'll soon have a resolution

When problems come, it's the Holy Spirit's job, to solve them

Yes, there are times you try to press forward without giving it to Him

Everything starts to falter when you get closest to destiny

But God is a present help in times of trouble

When pain comes, still worship and watch for the double

God is not a man He should lie

And Jesus only died once

When pain comes, just know here comes passion

And with passion here comes peace

My latter shall be greater than my former

Only if you believe and press towards greater heights

Jesus has paid the price for it all

Who was in much pain, but never did He fall

Keep looking to Jesus who is the Author and Finisher

Who is the Great Sustainer?

When pain comes just know

My destiny is greater, and God's glory shall show

Press, Press, Press, pass the pain

Because believe it or not, there is greater gain

HEAVENLY FATHER

When no one else was there

You were always there

When no one else understood me

You always knew me and understood me

When no one else could help me

You are my present help in trouble times

When no one seemed to love me

You were and is still loving me out of my mind

When all had talked about me

You were still encouraging me

When they were putting me down

You still were elevating me up without a sound

When they betrayed me and bruised my heart

You were still giving me a new start

When sickness and disease tried to overtake me

You were still proving you are Jehovah Rapha to me

When the collectors said you'll never be out of debt

You showed me as well as them, You are the Ruler, and

everything is set

When trouble seemed to be everywhere

You continually showed me a way of escape, a gift I can share

When the enemy was throwing all types of fiery darts

You equipped me with the shield of faith and gave me a new

start

When it seem you were far away

Zephaniah 3:17, declared you always rest in your love each and

every day

When it seems I could do no more

You continue to tell me to stand above and soar

When the world tells us all kinds of lies

You tell us to trust You because You are nigh

You never come to deceive

Father, I've made up my mind I'll believe the report of You

And your promise I will receive.

GROWN

A man does not teach another man

If he is still acting like a boy

A woman can not teach another woman

If she is still acting like a girl

Growth is the characteristic of righteousness

Not my own will of selfishness

People make the statement, "I'm Grown"

But you are not grown until you stop doing wrong

Every decision should be Lord what shall I say

Lord what shall I do, and Lord which way shall I go

A person that is grown first listens to instructions

Instructions of the Father's will and directions

What makes one think he/she is grown

Is it because you have something you own and doing your own thing?

No, grown is characterized by those who are responsible, persistent, diligent, and faithful

Who has love for the Father and the desire to please Him

Putting off concerning the old man deeds

Putting on the equipment of the new man and bearing fruitful seeds

God said its time to arise and shine

Stop thinking it is about you and your mind

But it is all about the Supreme God

Who is grown and complete, with wisdom, understanding, and knowledge

And has no one to compete?

So, the next time you say I'm Grown

Stop and think, is it about me or about God,

The true fruits that should be shown

Is He getting the glory out of your grown self?

If not, then you are still carnal, and your ears are still deaf

THINKING BEFORE ACTING

Wisdom will save us from the ways of wicked men

We should all take heed to what we tell kids and flee from sin

Counting to five before we react, we must ponder these

questions:

Is it right and will it teach a valuable lesson?

Is it good for the spirit or has it made my flesh feel good?

Is it helpful or are we speaking straight hood?

Would God approve this behavior?

Would my parents approve or even my Savior?

If the answer to any of these questions is no

Then it is imperative to stop counting and go

Go the other way before having to repent for doing wrong

With the Gospel knowledge, we are learning how to respond

even if it's a song

Just know God's wisdom will judge you accordingly

Because now we are dividing his word proportionally

God gave us instructions for every situation

We can't keep blaming people or getting entangled with the

participation

 Think before you act

If not, the way you act will prove how you think

N.O.W (NEVER OUT WAVERING)

Faith deposits manna of today

Hope follows faith to see what He says

Love says it is already there

Love also says I have a key to it all and am willing to share

Joy says if you're not happy it is because you have not found

your true strength

Peace you shall have if you keep your mind stayed on thee

Freeing one from worry and fear without wavering

Longsuffering has to be patient with others because others need

to also be caring

Now is the time to enact the fruit of the Spirit

Life is more than hearing the lyrics

Lyrics can sometimes have us wavering in the sea

The Word of God will have us standing on what we believe

TRUST

You said you trust me to be your Provider

But when the bills are due, you look for a honey or try to win

the lottery

You said you trust me to be your Healer,

But when sickness comes instead of getting addicted

to my word

You are addicted to medicines

You said you trust me to be your Shepherd,

But when trouble comes you leave and go to other masters

You said you trust me to be your Banner,

But when the enemy comes in like a flood, you let him stay in

You said you trust Me to be your Peace,

But you allow your flesh to be at war like a raging sea

You said you trust Me to be your Help,

But you keep running from Me when I come to correct

You said you trust Me to be your Guide,

But you always going trying to sneak and to hide

You said you trust me to be your Righteousness,

But every time I turn around you bring shame and acting

Christ-less

You said you trust me to be more than enough,

But you never give me your tithes before the unnecessary stuff

It is easy to say the word "trust"

But your actions tell Me if you really do or don't trust Me

Stop, think, do you really trust Me with your actions

Or is it just lip motions

You said you trust Me, now show Me

CHOICE

We have no choice in the time of birthing

We have no choice of our gender behind the curtaining

We have no choice where we shall call home

To be murdered, fostered, adopted, or left alone

We have no choice of our skin color

We have no choice to be short or taller

We have no choice regarding the things that are not in our

hand

But we do have a choice and a decision to be a better man

I have a choice to live or die

I have a choice to be happy or to cry

I have a choice who my company shall be

I have a choice to be bound or free

I have a choice who I need to conversate to

I have a choice to just sit or to get up and do

I have a choice to spend time wisely or foolishly

I have a choice to speak nasty or pleasantly

Whatever you are comfortable doing or taking

Ask yourself what choice am I really making

I have no choice who to love

Because that is the law and God choice above

But I do have a choice who's in my space

Because if you're not speaking life you have to make haste

Always know we have to make choices in life

Some will bless you and some will cause you to die

Make the right choice with Christ being first in your life

And, you will never intentionally make the wrong choice in His

sight

WHERE WOULD I BE, WHERE WOULD I GO

Where would I be

Where would I go

If Christ had not died for me

Where would I be

Where would I go

If the Blood could not have sustained me

Where would I be

Where would I go

If Jesus didn't redeem me

Where would I be

Where would I go

If Jesus did not reconcile me

Where would I be

Where would I go

If Jesus had not come to seek and save me

Where would I be

Where would I go

If God was not so rich in mercy towards me

Where would I be

Where would I go

If God didn't give a measure of faith to me

Where would I be

Where would I go

If God only looked at the old instead of the new me

Where would I be

Where would I go

If God didn't have His own purpose and plan for me

Where would I be

Where would I go

If Holy Spirit did not guide me

Where would I be

Where would I go

If the Comforter did not abide forever with me

Where would I be

Where would I go

If the Interpreter did not speak with boldness through me

Where would I be

Where would I go

If the Revealer did not reveal the truth to me

Where would I be

Where would I go

If my Friend was not always with me

I would be lost, afflicted, confused, and in despair

I would go to hell, fire, pit, and be in torment

I'm so glad I know the Father (Trinity) loves me

And has proven His love towards me

That is the reason you still see me

Where would I be and where would I go-

so thankful that I am free

WHO AM I

Who Am I

Who Am I

Who Am I

I know whose I am

But what purpose am I here for

Who Am I

You are a child of the Most High

Favorable in the sight of God

To do and willing to do

The assignment God has for you

Who Am I

I am a bearer of light

I am a bearer of unity

I am a bearer of strength

I am a bearer of wisdom

I am a bearer of understanding

I am a bearer of peace

I am a bearer of long-suffering

I am a bearer of compassion

I am a bearer of joy

I am a bearer of gentleness

I am a bearer of goodness

I am a bearer of meekness

I am a bearer of self-control

I am a bearer and structure of faith

I am the greatest love gift any man has seen

From the DNA of my Father

Without love, everything is only noise

Not even compared to those 12 disciple boys

Jesus left us Great Holy Spirit

That will direct us if only we submit

I am a new creature

Everything old about me has passed away

Look, now everything and all things are become new

Who Am I

I house the Spirit of the Living God

Before the foundations of the world was, I was there

Who Am I

The vessel my Father use to get His work done

That's who I am

A child of the Most High

To bring the Great I am Glory

Loved of my Father

The apple of His eye

That's who I am

Give praise to Holy Spirit for directing us where we are

Jesus for bringing us into what we are

God for creating us for who we are

That's who we are

The Creation and a child of the Living God

Never let anyone devalue your gift

The Gifter is inside of His gifts to shift

Woe to every man that rises against us

You just condemn your own selves

I know Who I Am

And my Father always sees about me

MY HUSBAND

Having one child out of wedlock seemed wild

Who is the man that will marry me, hand to hand

I felt all my life was a mess and a shame

Didn't even understand the game

August 1997, I met this handsome guy

So, I acted and seemed like I was shy

Because I didn't know or read God's plan

A man that findeth a wife findeth a good thang

As years passed by

In 1998, here am I, birthing Ty

By the one I called my friend, my love

That always treated me sweet as a dove

December 1998, I married this guy

the one that adamantly calls me his wife

June 1999, I found my Great Savior

As my husband and I shared matrimony

We also shared a great born-again testimony

Someone like myself

I found greatness and greatness found me

Now the life I live with my loving husband is sweet as an apple

tree

God allowed us to bear the purpose of four children

One that died in the womb of his woman

We never truly understand God's plan

But always make Him the first MAN

He will direct you in every area

Especially in the area that seemed that couldn't be shared

He will grant you with the best earthly friend, lover, and

husband

That sometimes may not understand all of you

But God always choose what is best for me and is true

My husband has allowed God to lead the way

Now he is always taking my hand, or standing, kneeling to

pray

He never ceases to anoint my head

Or making sure no ill feelings bear our bed

He even covers me in prayer before preaching

Who would have thought this and he isn't a deacon

He never ceases to say I love you

Every day is not a bed of roses

But we learned to cut the stem and put in the hoses

Whatever we can't overcome

We trust the Master to get things done

It truly takes three in a marriage

Getting rid of any and all outsiders

Bringing a family into this world is not a joke

Both parties have to trust God and continue to seek hope

Thankful for my husband and friend

We choose to live the abundant life and refuse to sin

We have been through a cadre of problems

Nothing Holy Spirit can not do to help resolve them

We are thankful for this walk with Him

He has taught us how to shine and never be dim

It was in devotion we asked God to restore and reset any

convictions

And we wait for Him to reveal the manifestations

We don't sit and regurgitate our pain

And we refuse to allow others to do the same

God had divinely connected this spiritual partnership

And we are thankful for the Godly relationship

We know what it means when people say a true love story

never ends

When we thought it was over it was God who was able to

mend

We are a living testimony and thankful for everything God sent

His love will cause us to be strong and never bend

Trust His way at all times

DON'T SHED A TEAR FOR ME

Don't shed a tear for me

Just know I've gone to be with family

I was only here to love you a little while

But to love my Father as a child

Time has finally come for me to go

But I pray I lived to show one the right road

So, don't shed a tear for me my dear

Just know God is always near

He said He'll never leave you

Nor will He ever forsake you

Cleave to the Almighty's great hand

Never put your trust in any man

So, whatever you're feeling at this time

Just remember to keep God on your mind

For He is the keeper of your soul

He doesn't want you to be left out of the fold

Seek God while He is near

For He loves you greater my dear

So, don't shed a tear for me

Just know I've gone to be with family

So, don't shed a tear in grief for me

But praise God continually

For He loves you best my dear

In Loving Memory of my Dad February 15, 2016

WAS IT JUST A DREAM?

As the days and nights went by, I would question myself, was it just a dream?

A dream of loving you all through the night

Never wanting to depart, always keeping you in my sight

Was it just a dream when my heart failed head over heels for you?

As you took my breath away with each kiss that felt so true

Was it just a dream when I couldn't even stand up straight?

Or waiting anxiously for you at the gate

Was it just a dream knowing my mind was consciously on you?

Was it just a dream when I touched your body feeling so true?

Was it just a dream when I was told to walk away?

Was it just a dream when God constantly told me to pray?

Only God knows the plans He has for us all

Especially me due to my appointed call

In life I never imagined I could love someone so deeply

But he wasn't like the others ... knowingly

It seemed like a love that was organic

One that would make a girl go manic

It had been years since my heart had been set free

He showed me love and good times even under the tree

Missing him like crazy had become a part of my life

But I didn't want to interfere with any strife

Was it just a dream that I wanted him here with me?

Was it just a dream to realize he weren't free?

Out of all the things we have tried to force

Love will and never be forced due to it being a given choice

Some people like their security blanket and that's ok

The blanket that one really doesn't like but that's familiar – I'll

just say

Was it just a dream when I sensed him unhappy?

No one to challenge or pressure him, so he stayed with the

crappy

Crappy life of comfortability

Not taking one ounce of accountability

At one point his heart was what I was after

Although others were thirsty for the package that matter

He liked to run life with other girls

Yet, I refuse to go around in those same swirls

When one truly loves someone there are no uncertainties

We learn to catapult one another to completely different

personalities

Was it just a dream that he were the man I was seeking after?

Was it just a dream that I was force-feeding

him to love me later?

I wanted this reciprocal determinism

But most just only think about getting an orgasm

Was it just a dream the night we talked each other to sleep?

Was it just a dream listening to music

showing each other a peep?

I prayed and asked God to really show me the right way

This is what He had to say

Daughter, you are the apple of my eye

You don't get leftovers, not even from a pie

Never will I leave you the crumbs,

not even the partial fragments

I will never allow mine to be an option or

a debate of who's better

It wasn't a dream that you were about to

be someone's second choice

Even though you knew you were the better voice

Voice of reasoning, the voice of seasoning, boy,

I'd have him dreaming

Yes, finding all the ways we could be sex scheming

Man, it would have been the unforgivable sin

But God's love is greater than any man, penis, or den

Be careful that you don't become

a comparison or a competition

Just remember, God will pull you out of the race

of their superstition

His glory, anointing, purpose, fulfillment,

will never be seen in another

Rest in knowing that God knows you better than you know

your own brother

He knows better than you and can see beyond the future

God will give us better than what we

can ever imagine my sister

Trust His ways better than you can even phantom

Was it just a dream that I love hard even like Samson?

Was it just a dream that I love one even before time?

Was it just a dream that he were not my prime?

God knows what's in store for us especially me

And I trust Him to allow me to be at peace

Was it just a dream?

Was it just a dream?

YOU GOT DISS, SIS

You got diss, sis

Because he didn't think you were the one

You got diss, sis

Because he wanted to run and still have fun

You got diss, sis

Because he thought she was better

You got diss, sis

Because he couldn't make up his mind

You got diss, sis

Because everyone else was the priority

You got diss, sis

Because she had bigger breast

You got diss, sis

Because she had smaller breast

You got diss, sis

Because she had wider hips

You got diss, sis

Because she looked like a toothpick

You got diss, sis

Because she had longer hair

You got diss, sis

Because she had shorter hair

You got diss, sis

Because she was shaped like a coke bottle

You got diss, sis

Because he can't make up his mind while still lying

You got diss, sis

Because you were still an option

You got diss, sis

Because he was still a child playing games

You got diss, sis

Because he refuses to grow up and become a man

You got diss, sis

Because he cut more grass than mow his own

You got diss, siss

Because he still wants to act like a fool in school

You got diss, sis…. and that wasn't cool

But did you really?

Nah, you woke up

He was dissing his so-called Ms./Mrs./Miss, and you

And was ready to run with the next one too

What felt like a diss

Was just his missed opportunity

Never think for one second that you got dissed

It was God protecting you with His kiss

Kiss that mess goodbye and be thankful for what might have felt like a lie

Don't be distracted by the dis-ease of man's mind

That is not what God promised, he is not your kind

In all actuality, it was a dis-connection to those not worth your time or energy

Keep moving sis, we have more territory to dis-mantle and dis-miss.

He can keep all his dis-respect

And give it to his own pet

OH GIRL, YOU ARE POWERFUL

When the enemy comes to hurt us

God comes to hear, heal, and deliver us

I know that I am here to empower women

And to allow those women to empower other women

The most important stage in any babe's life… is the early stages

So, when we meet, just know we are not meeting for anything

But preparing for something of His choice

Never let anyone cause you to sacrifice your voice

Our society have taught our young girls and older

That likeability is an essential part of who we are

To twist ourselves in so many shapes to make others like us

Hold back how you feel

Pull back if you want a deal

Stay quiet, don't be pushy, and don't be so aggressive

Why? So, others can run over us like water pressure

I was not created to be likable

But I was created to shine my light

Never subject yourself to be someone's "liking" puppet

Moving, doing, and saying only at the sound of trumpets

We live in a diverse and multi-faceted place

Make sure everyone knows your face

You may not say a single word

But know when we show up...... just know we will be heard

You want me to be quiet because I might offend

That is good, so now I don't have to pretend

Just know your story has a purpose and it has a sound

No more walking around with a frown

Find your voice to make the sound that heaven wants to hear

And watch all of hell fear

Oh girl, you are powerful

And yes, you are very colorful

Never let anyone tell you your crayons are no good

Even the broken ones can change a mood as they should

Let your light shine whether someone says it is bright or not

The light knows what it was designed to do without an extra

plot

A star never has to question its ability

Whether the clouds hover over it or not, it never diminishes its

capability

Oh, girl, YOU ARE POWERFUL

MAIN DISH

So many of us have been so satisfied eating off other people's plate

Not putting any spiritual time in,

And now our spirit is at stake

Some come to worship service

Ready to eat off Pastor's plate

Not even having a mind to seek God and always come to church late

May find a few minutes to hear Sunday school

Yep, now you are ready to eat all of the deacon's food

May even have a call to teach the youth

Not seeking God for what He wants to speak in all His truth

God has placed our own plate in front of us

Sadly, you haven't touched your food, but ready to fuss

Fuss with what is or isn't on the plate

But haven't even given God any time but wonder about your fate

Not eating what is required so now you question your purpose

Every purpose, every will, every plan, every vision, is with those who are tenacious

What are we doing to fulfill what is being given to us

Understandably, not everyone will have the same meal plan

In the devotional times, when we study and commune with God,

we'll understand His hand

We may have the same veggies or sides alike

But the main course meal comes from Him regarding what He likes

He knows what we have need of,

and when we need it

Allow Him to prepare the main dish of all your needs

If not, you will be spiritually malnourished, and never be able to lead

MY BEAUTIFUL SKIN

All throughout Scriptures, we are reminded not to fear

Why, because God is with us even when we shed one tear

Let me remind you that when God creates something

You never have to fear the outcome because false evidence is

nothing

He will always have our best interest at heart

He will work it together for our good just like the start

He created you in the beautiful image of your skin

Never let anyone diminish you or make you feel less than

Refuse to be ashamed of your complexion

Do not dare compare or be any man's collection

We are fearfully and wonderfully made

Even if my skin turns shades

We are beautiful black beings

Regardless, of how one holds their internal sins

Why do people want us to question who and what we are?

Baby, you are looking at a golden star

God never makes any mistakes

Not even when He birthed you different from the fakes

Before the foundation of the world was, we were there

Stand bold in who you are because you are an heir

I know, I am an heir of God and joint-heir of Jesus that care

That lets me know there is no other man that can repair

Oh, beautiful skin be proud of who you are

Never distort your color like a beautiful star

Walk with your head high

When others see you that have to sigh

Hold your shoulders straight

Be you, walk true, and don't dare be a fake

Speak with the voice of knowledge

Because you know that your God has a hedge of prowess

A hedge of protection on you beautiful

Never fear but do what is always suitable

Oh, beautiful skin

You are more than your skin and the looks of men

You are valuable from the inner being

If only others would take the time and really start living

Oh, beautiful skin

Know who you are so you never have to pretend

SHIKWON

You are my oldest and firstborn

Many days I didn't know how you were going to form

I was doing things that I shouldn't have done

But thankfully I made the decision to give up the fun

Son, you were the child that saved my life

Often, I tried to destroy my life but knew I had to fight

I was fighting for every generation curse to be over

Even the days I felt like I was ran over by a bulldozer

Many nights I cried and wondered why

Why things were happening like they were, Shi

I know that your dad died at a young age

But God graced you with a dad that wouldn't let you stay in

rage

Tears of grief streamed down your face

Oftentimes, allowing you to do things that were a disgrace

God knows the plans He has for us all

Even when we do things that cause us to fall

Son, our bond runs deep

It was you that helped me off the streets

I know that I wanted to show you a better life

That is why I had to let go of all the unnecessary strife

If truth be told, a lot of things I wasn't happy about

But today we can both lift our hands and shout

God has a way of bringing us out

Only to those that are willing to believe and never doubt

I will forever show you God's way

He is the only thing that I know each and every day

Son whatever gift lies within you this day

Never put a muzzle over it, but speak up and say

Say what God has placed on your heart

Even when the enemy comes with his fake darts

Be all God has called you to be

Always live the best life and be free

Freedom can only be given from one

And that's the gift of God's only Son

Love you always and forever, Shikwon

DORIEON

When I found out I was pregnant with you

I cried because I didn't think it was true

How can I be pregnant yet again?

Falling in the trap of another sin

I wanted to be married by the time I gave birth

I was tired of going around the same test on this earth

Falling for men that I thought were for me

Knocking me up and then leaving me to be

Be the mother of their children

Not knowing what the outcome was I started fearing

Fearing that I was going to fall into another trap

But what I didn't know was God had plans amid the gap

Those gaps were preparing us to be a family

One thing I know about you, you love family and Zaxby

When you were born you came out in no time

Man, I thought your dad would pass out because of the slime

You were a 9 pounder

Boy, your head was a heavy weightier

Oftentimes, I look at you now and wonder

How I birth something so tall and handsome, and yet so tender

Your heart is tender to love each and every person

Even when they treat you like crap, but you never immerse or

curse them

You smile and walk away

Because you know that is the best way

You are a true leader

Even when you only have one cheerleader

You have learned that God is the best audience

With him, you will never have to glut for applauses

Continue to shine bright for the Master

He has so much in store for you just like your Pastor

Move with Him, for Him, and then watch Him

Do the impossible in your life without scheming

Love you always and forever, Dorieon

SHADAESHA

Our first little girl

What will we name her, Cheryl

Nah that just didn't suit you

I wanted a name from the Bible one that was true

So I named you Nehemiah but spelled Nehemya

While carrying you I was prophesied that you will be a gift of

fire

Fire in your mouth to speak that of truth

One that will pull up every false root

When you were born

I had complications so I had to be torn

You wanted to come out arms first

I had to have an emergency cesarean so it was hard to nurse

You had hair all over you that was formed

And a cry that sounded like a horn

You were one of the most beautiful babies I had ever seen

Beautiful complexion as the sun beamed

 Growing up you never gave me any trouble

As you sat and watched your cartoons *Dora Explorer*

You would sit in your reclining chair

And you would stay right there

Even days when I had to do hair

You would be so content in your little purple chair

As long as you had a snack you would be ok

Never mumbled a word or had anything to say

You are very reserved even today

Only speaking what is necessary and benefiting to say

You are a true godly introvert

Thankfully, with Him, you never convert

Never convert to how people want you to be

That is the only way to stay and be free

Free to please the Father and never man

Man with mixed feelings- one day liking you and the next day,

they can't stand

Be true to yourself and who you are

Never devalue yourself or steep to their bar

You are very atypical indeed

But never run in the race of others speed

You are our beautiful little girl

With the darkest hair and beautiful curls

Continue to be the threshing instrument that can see souls

Discerning the one that is fake and the one that glows

Love you always and forever, Shadaesha

DESTINY

You were destined to be here

Because we definitely didn't plan for you, my dear

You were a surprise indeed

Because your dad had already dispelled all his seeds

When I felt a little funny

I went to the doctor and there you were, honey

Baking in the oven

I was told they were 2 minus a dozen

I was a little fearful because I was just getting my life together

Well, I thought I was getting it together just a little better

Mom went through some stressful events before your entrance

Wanted to make sure we were ready for your appearance

Your dad and I was on the verge of divorce

But here you come as another source

I guess it was God's way of saying to stay together

But I had my mind made-up I wasn't going to be shifted like

any weather

After I gave birth to you, I wanted to take you home for sure

You were so beautiful and so pure

Home maybe a week and then I was right back at the hospital

Didn't know what was going on but had to undergo double

bypass myocardial

What in the world just happened

At home, loving my baby and in the ambulance was I fastened

It was a shocker to us all

No warning signs, not even a chance, to make a call

Even after staying in the hospital away from my family and

baby

I finally came home, and right back they had to take me

I had a thrombus two inches from my heart

Now I'm depressed and feel like I don't know how to start

How can I start to build a relationship with my baby girl

I'm back in the hospital head spinning like a swirl

Attacked from every angle

But you were a good baby and strong like a wonderful angel

You are my strong social butterfly

Never allowing anything to break you or make you cry

Love you always and forever, Destiny

DON'T TRY IT

When we try to make a man like God

It will never work because there is only one and true living God

Who is like Him

Who can compare to Him

Earthly man will only fleshly love you but before the world

was; He was

He is the Great King and the wonderful Lord

A man can emulate Him but could never be Him

His love is never fading

He won't love you today, and throw you away by tomorrow

Even if He gets mad, He will not allow anger to control His

motives

Why are we trying to expect a man to be like our God

Even in the midst of pain only He can comfort

Man is supposed to do according to what they have seen and

heard to now do

This doesn't make you God but a little god

Doing only what the Father has said and proved

Yet, many focus on self and forget what He has spoken

Don't try to make a man like God

It is impossible

I SHOULDN'T HAVE TO QUESTION LOVE

What is love?

Can you see it?

Can you describe it?

Can you taste it?

Can you make love to it?

Just what is true love?

Whatever it may be you shouldn't have to question it

It comes from the very spiritual being of God

He is love and for us to understand that love we must

understand Him

His love is unconditional

His love is everlasting

His love is never wavering

His love is genuine

His love is organic

I never have to question His love

Oftentimes we question love because it is not seen

He says, he loves you with his lips but actions questions that

love

She says I love you with her lips but actions questions that love

I shouldn't have to question love

The feelings of deep affection should prove love

Every interest in loving me should prove love

The sweetness of pleasure to me should prove love

The yearning to be like the Creator should show you love me

God never questioned if Jesus loved Him because He proved it

He was willing to sacrifice His life for a world that wouldn't do

the same

Jesus stepped down from glory so we can step up to the

Kingdom

He left His Kingdomship to help us gain a relationship

Bore the pain of the cross

Because His love was wrapped and nailed in obedience

God, not for one second, questioned His Son's love

You shouldn't have to question if you are loved or not

Evidence will prove love in full force

Knowledge will prove love in full force

Identity will prove love in full force

Obedience will prove love in full force

Submission will prove love in full force

Relationship will prove love in full force

Faith will prove love in full force

Sacrifice will prove love in full force

Whenever we find ourselves questioning love

We need to stop, step back and ask ourselves, am I distributing

Kingdom love

If I am, it shall and will come back to me

Everyone is not set out to love you, but those who do

Shouldn't and wouldn't have to be questioned

1 John 3:13 says, "marvel not, my brethren, if the world hate

you"

Understand they are doing their job, but your job requires you

to love them

Don't allow someone to question your love

The same way we shouldn't have to question others

Others shouldn't have to question our love either

Why?

Because we are the ones who have learned true love by way of

our First Love

No one should have to question love if it comes from above

About the Author

C.L. Suggs (Carlesha) grew up in the small country of Pink Hill, NC, where at an early age, she first began to write poetry as a means of expressing and understanding her feelings during her time of traumatic events. She was inspired by her late grandmother Catherine Kinsey who would stand up in church without any paper and recite poems that were in her heart. That always amazed C.L. but she could only find enjoyment when she wrote out the poems because of all her anxieties and delays. Many thought it would be impossible with the adverse trauma that she endured, that she wouldn't even be able to function in life. Yet, her words are expressed with the love of her Heavenly Father who reconstructed what man thought couldn't be.

She is the author of several books including Unlocking Mysteries in the Kingdom, Abused, Afflicted, Confused, but now Delivered, and Real Evolution Heals. She has been through a heap of dilemmas in her lifespan, but through each experience, it taught her how to deal with the pain. She takes no credit for the healing; she gives it all to Holy Spirit in all wisdom. She learned to collaborate with Spirit, and He has blessed her life tremendously in all areas. Holy Spirit is the fount life-giver of every blessing. She and her husband have together five children.

C.L. detested writing in school but God had need of her hands. She is not versed in all the various segments of poetry, but God is. So, whatever you read: listen, take heed, and be delivered through her thoughts and life that brought her clarity and answers in her own writing style. She is the founder of CRC Coaching School, to help others just like her, give birth to their dreams.

Other Books by C.L. Suggs

Unlocking Mysteries in the Kingdom
Abused, Afflicted, and Confused but now DELIVERED
Real Evolution Heals (R.E.H.) I had to become her, to realize, I wasn't her

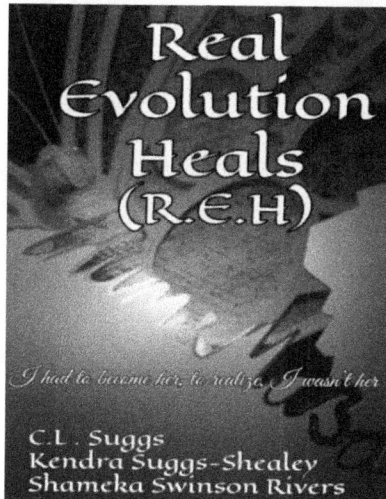

(with Kendra Shealey and Shameka Rivers)